Light
and
Darkness

Light
and
Darkness

By FRANKLYN M. BRANLEY

Illustrated by REYNOLD RUFFINS

Thomas Y. Crowell Company · New York

LET'S-READ-AND-FIND-OUT SCIENCE BOOKS

Editors: *DR. ROMA GANS*, Professor Emeritus of Childhood Education, Teachers College, Columbia University
DR. FRANKLYN M. BRANLEY, Astronomer Emeritus and former Chairman of The American Museum-Hayden Planetarium

* Available in Spanish

Copyright © 1975 by Franklyn M. Branley   •   Illustrations copyright © 1975 by Reynold Ruffins

Library of Congress Cataloging in Publication Data Branley, Franklyn Mansfield. Light and Darkness. SUMMARY: Discusses the properties of light, particularly its source in heat. 1. Light—Juvenile literature. [1. Light] I. Ruffins, Reynold, ill. II. Title. QC360.B7   535   74-23938   ISBN 0-690-00704-3   ISBN 0-690-00705-1 (lib. bdg.)

1   2   3   4   5   6   7   8   9   10

Light
and
Darkness

In the morning when you get up there is
sunlight. Maybe it's cloudy and you can't see the
sun. But it really is shining. If you were flying
above the clouds you could see the sun.

In the daytime there is light. That's because the
sun is shining on your part of the earth.

1

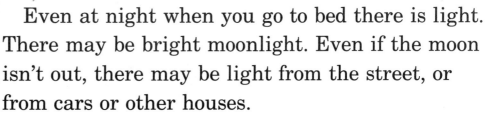

Even at night when you go to bed there is light. There may be bright moonlight. Even if the moon isn't out, there may be light from the street, or from cars or other houses.

All the time there is light around you.

When it's dark inside, you turn on a light.

When it's dark outside, the streetlights come on. Or you turn on your flashlight.

Even when all these lights are off, there is still some light. It's hard to find a place that is really dark.

Sunlight comes from the sun. The sun is very hot. It sends out light to us.

Starlight comes from the stars. The stars, too, are very hot. They send out light to us.

Light comes from things that are very hot. The flame of a candle is hot. The little bulb in a flashlight is hot. And the big bulb in a lamp is hot. We call these hot things light sources, because light comes from them. They must be very hot to make light.

We can see things that are hot enough to make light. We see the sun, the stars, the candle flame, the light bulb. They are good light sources.

Suppose you were in a dark room, so dark there was no light at all. And suppose there were some way you could heat a nail to make it get hotter and hotter. The nail would get so hot it would produce light. There would be a red glow in the room. When it got hotter, the nail would produce

yellow light, and then light that was almost white. The hotter it got, the more light it would make. That is just what happens inside an electric light bulb. When you turn the switch, little wires inside the bulb get hot. They get so hot that they send out a lot of light.

We see things when they get hot enough to make light. We also see things that light falls upon. Most of the things that we see—chairs, people, trees, grass, rocks, books—are not hot. They do not send out their own light. We see

them because light falls on them, light that comes from the sun, or a candle, or a light bulb. It comes from a light source, something that is hot. The light comes straight from the source. It travels in straight lines.

When light falls on something, it bounces off again, like a rubber ball. When light bounces off something, we say it is reflected, or turned around. It is turned and sent in a different direction. When light is turned and sent to us, we see whatever is reflecting that light.

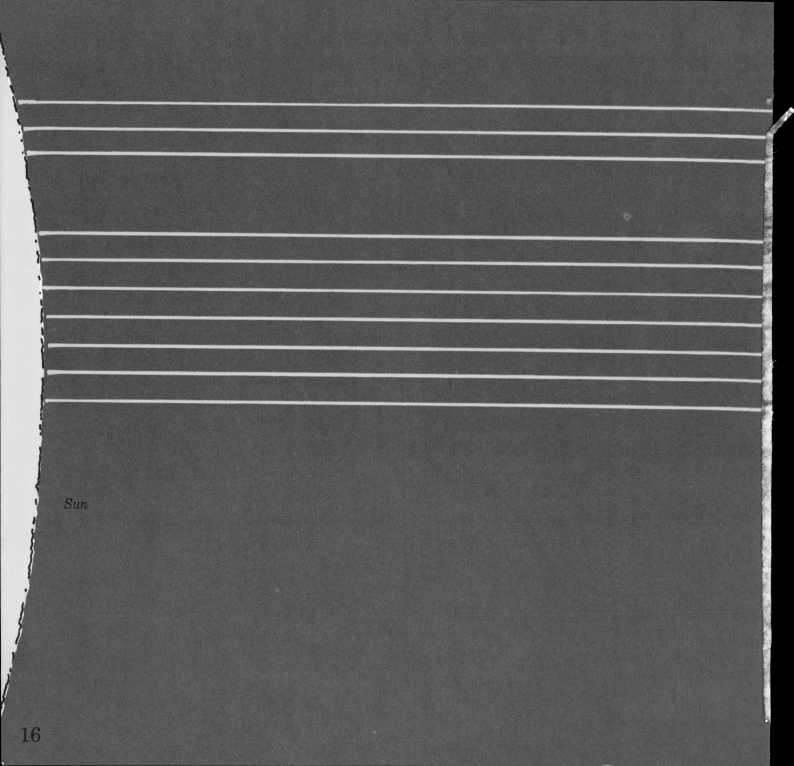

Sun

16

Moon

Earth

We see trees, grass, and rocks because sunlight falls on them. They reflect sunlight to us. We see the moon because sunlight falls on it. The moon reflects sunlight to us. The moon really does not make moonlight. Moonlight is reflected sunlight.

Light from the sun falls on Venus and Mars and the other planets. The planets are not hot like stars. They are not light-makers. We see the planets because they reflect sunlight to us. Astronauts in space see the earth because the earth reflects sunlight to them.

Look around you. How many things do you see
that send out their own light? If it is daytime,
you will probably see only one—the sun. If it is
night, you will also probably see only one
kind—light bulbs. Or it could be a candle flame or
a flashlight or the stars.

How many things do you see that *reflect* light?
Probably hundreds of them. We see most things
because they reflect light.

Light travels very fast. You can see this when you turn on a lamp at night. All at once the whole room is filled with light. Suppose you were in a great big room, a room as big as the Astrodome. The same thing would happen. If the light were big enough and bright enough, all at once the whole great big room would be filled with light. Point a flashlight at a tree far away. As soon as you turn on the light, you can see the tree.

Light travels so fast it can go to the moon and back in three seconds. If you could travel that fast you could go around the world seven times in one second.

Light is just about everywhere. Probably you've
never been anywhere where there wasn't some
light.

A dark room seems very dark, at first. But after
a while you can see things because there is always
a little light in every room. Try this experiment:

Take a white dish into a room and put it down. Then turn out the light. At first you won't see the dish. That's because your eyes have to get used to the darkness. You will see more and more as the pupils, or openings, in your eyes get larger.

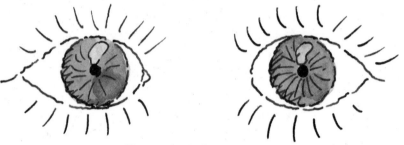

Your eyes in bright light

Pretty soon you may see the white dish. Pull the shades all the way down to make it darker. You may still be able to see a little bit. Maybe you can't see the dish. But you can probably see where the windows are.

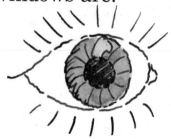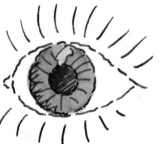

Your eyes in dim light

27

It would be darker under your bed covers on a dark night. Or maybe inside a dark closet in a dark room on a dark night. Maybe there would be no light at all. That would be real darkness.

There would be real darkness in a cave deep under the ground. Or a cellar with no windows would be really dark. If you were inside a big metal ball it would be dark. Maybe you can think of other places where it would be really dark.

Our world is full of light that comes to us from things that are hot. Most of our light comes from the hot sun. But we get some light from other hot things—candles, lamps, and electric lights.

All during the day there is sunlight, even on a cloudy day. During the day your half of the earth is lit by the sun. At night, too, the earth is lit by the sun. People say it is lit by moonlight. But you know that the moon does not make its own light—moonlight is reflected sunlight. Almost everything we see—books, trees, houses, cars, people, bugs, birds, cats, and dogs—reflects light to us. Without light we could see nothing at all.

Moon

Sunlight

Earth

33

ABOUT THE AUTHOR

Franklyn M. Branley, Astronomer Emeritus and former Chairman of The American Museum-Hayden Planetarium, is well known as the author of many books about astronomy and other sciences for young people of all ages. He is also coeditor of the Let's-Read-and-Find-Out Science Books.

Dr. Branley holds degrees from New York University, Columbia University, and the State University of New York College at New Paltz. He and his wife live in Woodcliff Lake, New Jersey.

ABOUT THE ILLUSTRATOR

Reynold Ruffins was born in New York City and educated at Cooper Union. He is the coauthor and illustrator of three innovative handbooks for children—on bicycles, chess, and codes and ciphers, as well as a book of riddles. His work has appeared in a wide variety of magazines, including *Family Circle*, *Cosmopolitan*, and *Fortune*, and has won awards from the Society of Illustrators, the Art Directors Club, and the American Institute of Graphic Arts. Mr. Ruffins is an adjunct professor of art at Syracuse University. He enjoys sailing and traveling whenever possible; he has gone camping in Canada and across the United States. With his wife and four children he now lives in New York City.